Table of content

- Introduction .... page 2
- Definition .... page 3
- How to play .... page 4
- Puzzles .... page 7
- Hints .... Page 91
- Solutions .... page 99

Introduction

You probably spend at least a couple of hours each week training your body--doing cardio, weight training, or even just walking. You're training your muscles to stay pliant and strong, your joints to stay fluid, and your body's physical systems to run optimally.

But how much time do you spend training your brain?

Brain training isn't a new concept. It can help us retain information, recall facts more quickly, and sharpen our focus. Even a brief course of brain exercises can help older adults improve reasoning skills and processing speed for 10 years after the training ends.

So give your brain a daily workout to sharpen your focus and become more intelligent.

Definition

A cryptogram is an encoded statement that requires a degree of strategy to decode. The cryptograms found in this puzzle game use a 1-to-1 substitution cipher. For example all of the letter N's in a cryptogram might stand for the letter B in the decoded statement. Aside from letters nothing else in the statement has been changed, e.g. spacing and punctuation. In the case of this puzzle game all statements are quotes from relatively famous to very famous individuals. Using your knowledge of the English language and grammar, see if you can decode the quote!

Cryptograms based on quotes are also commonly called cryptoquotes. The cryptoquotes found in this puzzle game are a mix of modern and historical quotes.

How to play?

How to Solve Cryptograms

Solving cryptograms is one of the more popular word games. Most cryptograms are simply encoded with single-transposition keys, where one letter is substituted for another. This seems to create complete gibberish on a screen, such as:

"Ygua ua gpq smtpmr xsm zrsem gpq yp apzbr xetoyphesna."

However, there are actually very clear and deliberate ways to figure out exactly what letters are substituted and the meaning of the cryptogram. The key, so to speak, is to look at some of the conventions of the English language and play a game of percentages and educated guesses.

Look for Common Letters

The first step is to realize that the most common letters in the English language are E, T, A, O, and N, with I and S a close second. So, the first step to solving the puzzle is to look at what letters occur most often in the above gibberish, and work with them.

M, R, and S appear three or four times each. Now, you can begin the process of trial and error by substituting the popular letters for the common ones. Simply replacing the letters and looking for patterns that remind you of common English words is a way to start.

Solve the Short Words

This is especially effective for short words that have only two or three letters.

- The most common two letter words are: OF, TO, IN, IS, IT, AS, HE, BE, BY, ON, OR, and AT.
- For three letters, it gets a little more complicated: AND and THE lead the list, with FOR, HIS, NOT, BUT, YOU, ARE, HER, and HAD coming after.

However, there are quite a few other three-letter words - for example (and to provide a hint to the solution) the three-letter words in the above cryptograph are actually "CAN" and "HOW" (one of them, GPQ, appears twice).

Spot the Repeated Letters

Other conventions of the English language can also provide clues. Only a few letters are actually ever repeated twice in a word: RR, LL, NN, MM, and fewer of these are in small words. So if there is a three-letter word containing repeating letter, such as SZZ, that word is almost certainly the word ALL. Another very common pattern is the letters TH - appearing in both THE and THAT, as well as THIS, THOSE, THEM, and more.

Look for Digraphs

To give another hint, in the above cryptogram the first word is "THIS." The technical term for two-letter combinations that commonly appear in the English language is digraphs. The most common digraphs are TH, HE, AN, IN, ER, RE, ES, ON, EA, and TI (this last is especially useful in discovering the common four-letter word ending -TION).

Knowing that gives a very powerful tool in figuring out the rest of the words. Since the first word is "THIS," and the letter combination YG (which you now know is TH) doesn't appear at the beginning of any other words, you know that none of them are words with TH at the beginning.

Go for the Unusual

Knowing what the words can't be is sometimes as useful as knowing what they can be. Also, knowing unusual words, such as those that begin with X can give you a great advantage in solving cryptograms.

Don't Overlook the Obvious

Other conventions of cryptographic puzzles are also useful to know. Sometimes, for example, they try to throw in non-transposed letters, so that ALL would be encoded GLL and a person spends forever trying to figure out what the letter L represents (the answer being itself).

Many cryptographic phrases begin with phrases like "The best..." or "Some of the..." or "The only..." and knowing that can give you a few options to try right away.

Look for the Pattern

It all comes down to making systematic educated guesses until the pattern emerges. Usually after the vowels are figured out there is an acceleration as the phrase becomes clear. One frustrating problem can be a cryptogram with errors in it, whether grammatical, spelling, or an encoding error - however, that can be looked on as just another bit of the puzzle to figure out, above and beyond the basic cryptographic algorithm.

Using these step by step processes, you can figure out that the puzzle at the beginning of the article uses the following substitution cipher:

S V X F R D H G U K J Z N M P O W E A Y I B Q C T L A B C D E F G H I J K L M N O P Q R S T U V W X Y Z

Which, translated, reads: *"This is how anyone can learn how to solve cryptograms."*

Puzzles

1. CD FTUFWT ENT GUIPBCRK JUA DEN HUI'WW KU, KU ZU DEN BJEB HUI YER'B JTEN BJTV ERHVUNT. – VCYJTWT NICS

2. OCQSEQSD QR OCK CVAFKRO YUAE OCKAK QR, YCQJC QR HAUIVIMX OCK AKVRUS RU WKY KSDVDK QS QO. ~ CKSAX WUAF

3. OPEZOTPLEZCQ BZSO ZQ ENS STTCFE, QCE ZQ ENS PEEPZQVSQE. ~ VPNPEVP JPQRNZ

4. ZENX LSNT VPEJY JEBPQJ UD JEBPQJ XSPYQ'J LSNT ZENX. ~ JUR QSJTP

5. BS PMLLRE ZSV ZMEF GSC VSEJ, ISPRSBR RUIR KI VSEJKBO ZMEFRE. ~ RUSB PCIJ

6. T'O N IPJNU LJGTJFJP TH GBRW, NHC T KTHC UYJ YNPCJP T ZMPW, UYJ OMPJ T YNFJ MK TU. ~ UYMOND AJKKJPDMH

7. W KERWZ KVRM UVL JRSVZR ERWNPLQ LCEVFHC ZWHPS; PL LWXRM MGRWL,

KRLREZPUWLPVU, WUK CWEK GVEX. ~ SVNPU IVGRNN

---

8. AP RBCEM, XCWRQMPEVD, RBQR WNUUPWW CW RBP LPWNVR TK RBP QXTNER TK RCXP AP FNR CE QR ATLM, CEWRPQY TK RBP JNQVCRD TK RCXP AP FNR CE. ~ QLCQEQ BNKKCEIRTE

---

9. CDP HRD KI NKZDHKC, JBFQEKVKXRQWV QKPIVRQM WPH HRBDWBD. MEDF HK PKM HRD KI EWZH AKZL. ~ HWORH KXRVOF

---

10. MVU ECWF GWJPU OVUQU NAPPUNN PEXUN YUIEQU OEQD TN TC MVU HTPMTECJQF. ~ RTHJW NJNNEEC

11. ZVSH OXSW, OXLT JGF, EXHT OYRNVSP. ~ UTJJ MTAVR

12. A LHBHQ RXXT M KMP XVV AL IP 2OZ. LXR XLH. ~ CANN DMRHZ

13. PWXHX DHX LI BXMHXPB PI BFMMXBB. EP EB PWX HXBFAP IG VHXVDHDPEIL,

WDHC YIHU, DLC AXDHLELS GHIR GDEAFHX. ~ MIAEL VIYXAA

---

14. IQNRDGN ESLDK, FDNRQFZ CKDHCPKH. ~ HDCRDVEPH

---

15. OFCUC YX SA OYZC GAU QTO-VSB-BUYCB ZASAOASR. OFCUC YX OYZC GAU JAUH. VSB OYZC GAU DALC. OFVO DCVLCX SA AOFCU OYZC. ~ QAQA QFVSCD

---

16. EUJISLGN QO EZU JYQVQER EL SLGN ELDUEZUG ELSJGB J WLIILC FQOQLC. EZU

JYQVQER EL BQGUWE QCBQFQBAJV JWWLIKVQOZIUCEO ELSJGB LGDJCQXJEQLCJV LYHUWEQFUO. QE QO EZU PAUV EZJE JVVLSO WLIILC KULKVU EL JEEJQC ACWLIILC GUOAVEO.~JCBGUS WJGCUDQU

---

17. WYNDUWI UC QZPNUTHMZPMV DZPR UE VYH RUJURK UN UWNY CBZMM GYOC. ~ DKWPV EYPR

---

18. T UHAB YXI JFTOI AC DNOOIDD: GIGTOKYTAH, XKFG BAFU KHG KH

NHFILTYYTHR GIMAYTAH YA YXI YXTHRD WAN BKHY YA DII XKJJIH. ~ CFKHU EEAWG BFTRXY

---

19. EPKGR DIH LHJD YD DIKJ ZPZHGD CBDJ XPB KG DIH LHJD CTYWH UPA DIH GHMD ZPZHGD. ~ PCAYI QKGUAHX

---

20. SKJO PR RZWWURR? P OKPCH PO PR J NPAOZMU YV KJIPCF J VBJPM VYM OKU OKPCF OKJO XYZ JMU EYPCF; HCYSPCF OKJO PO PR CYO UCYZFK, OKJO XYZ KJIU

FYO OY KJIU KJME SYMH JCE J WUMOJPC RUCRU YV LZMLYRU. ~ NJMFJMUO OKJOWKUM

---

21. AUL CPCLV EHU GTROECD UA MBQGUOL, EXCLC QLC CTMXE XUOLD UA XQLI HULW. ~ SCDDTJQ DQPTEJX

---

22. D'IQ GQPNVQR WKPW PVZWKDVM DV GDLQ TUNWK KPIDVM YUBQX LNUB HPWDQVYQ PVR KPNR TUNS. ~ MNQM OQKNQVRW

23. H PXGAYXF DRX EGPBX WT RGAF JWAI UC JWAIHYK RGAF. ~ NGAKGAXD NXGF

---

24. CZ ZBQUP B JRZ RD NVPEUWZBWNJBM EMUEBMBZCRV ZR KBXU PEUWZBWNJBM MUPNJZP CV LRZK LNPCVUPP BVI DRRZLBJJ. ~ MRYUM PZBNLBWK

---

25. A NQJX SZJE DYBZHCY A UQPY LW NQJX. ~ DAUU MZKYC

16

26. RJNSPLRW NVH LPYCJLQ SPVH YCNL KCELDW PT KPNX YCNY WYEKD YP YCHJV ZPFW. ~ SNXKPXS TPVFHW

27. PGT BTMQ HI CISP WOQEIFQ, CISP WISMEMQIFQ. QUI ZGSJR EMF'Q KGEFK QG MUGZIS KGJR YGEFM GF PGT NTMQ HIYOTMI PGT UOCI O KGGR ERIO. PGT'SI KGEFK QG UOCI QG ZGSL JELI YSOVP QG HSEFK QUOQ ERIO QG QUI OQQIFQEGF GX WIGWJI. ~ UISH LIJJIUIS

17

28. XV PS PXK NES ESOGNH OKU ZXKUH JV SZBCJMSSH, PS'GS WJXKW NJ EOQS RSNNSG RAHXKSHH HAIISHH. ~ ZOGM ROGGO

---

29. KEN OMWK AOLMIKJFK KEAFC KM PM AB DMS BAFP DMSIWNUB AF J EMUN AW KM WKML PACCAFC. ~ HJIINF YSBBNKK

---

30. QNJD IGBENJG TWN ESG E BGW, HWV'D DUKVC TWN UELG XEVHGH. TWN FNJD BWVDKVNEXXT KVBSGEJG TWNS XGESVKVP, DUG OET TWN DUKVC, EVH

DUG OET TWN EMMSWEBU DUG WSPEVKYEDKWV. K'LG VGLGS RWSPWDDGV DUED. ~ KVHSE VWWTK

---

31. EDFFWEE FHJ UW HCCHNJWA NJ HJG UXHJFK VS KDIHJ BHUVX. CKWXW NE HBMHGE XVVI HC CKW CVR NJ WLWXG RDXEDNC. ~ HJAXWM FHXJWTNW

---

32. XSDGQR EWT MDPBDSQ TD WDQ MDONVYQ. ~ XVWWV SDPOQQA

---

33. MWK OKUZ QJ HJIM TRZEJDZ, HJIM TJIUEUZJDZ. ZVJ GWIYN EUD'Z PWEDP ZW UVWGJI PWYN BWEDU WD MWK FKUZ QJBRKUJ MWK VRHJ R PWWN ENJR. MWK'IJ PWEDP ZW VRHJ ZW GWIA YEAJ BIRXM ZW QIEDP ZVRZ ENJR ZW ZVJ RZZJDZEWD WC TJWTYJ. ~ VJIQ AJYYJVJI

---

34. RW GY GRP QUY UYKOQX KPJ FRPJX AW YFBZAIYYX, GY'OY DARPD QA UKLY HYQQYO HTXRPYXX XTVVYXX. ~ FKOI HKOOK

35. XFW ORBX ZOHRDXPQX XFZQJ XR NR ZE MRK EZQN MRKDBWTE ZQ P FRTW ZB XR BXRH NZJJZQJ. ~ CPDDWQ LKEEWXX

36. HZBD AWVXZBW ILZ XPW X VWL, MLC'D DTRCY ILZ TXSW OXCMWM. ILZ UZBD VLCDRCZXOOI RCVPWXBW ILZP OWXPCRCE, DTW QXI ILZ DTRCY, XCM DTW QXI ILZ XJJPLXVT DTW LPEXCRFXDRLC. R'SW CWSWP NLPELDDWC DTXD. ~ RCMPX CLLIR

37. XZUULXX UPR YL PJJPKRLA KR PRO YEPRUQ VM QZGPR IPYVE. JQLEL KX PIBPOX EVVG PJ JQL JVW KR LTLEO WZEXZKJ. ~ PRAELB UPERLFKL

---

38. IBSJXY WHM PSUNSBX MS HSX PSFTZAX. ~ IZHHZ BSUFXXD

---

39. H REIK ZSGZ HT H TGHOIM, H KVBOME'Z FIXFIZ ZSGZ. NBZ H REIK ZSI VEI ZSHEX H UHXSZ FIXFIZ HQ EVZ ZFLHEX. ~ WITT NIYVQ

40. EO KOOT CB ZPPOHC CJZC EO EBK'C ZDEZQU NZWO CJO GRLJC TOPRURBKU, CJZC EO'DD UPGOE FH GBQZDDQ UBNOCRNOU — FKTOGUCZKTRKL CJZC VZRDFGO RU KBC CJO BHHBURCO BV UFPPOUU, RC'U HZGC BV UFPPOUU. ~ ZGRZKKZ JFVVRKLCBK

---

41. U'C KEYZUYKLQ JXRJ ROEGJ XRDI EI NXRJ MLTRVRJLM JXL MGKKLMMIGD LYJVLTVLYLGVM IVEC JXL YEY-MGKKLMMIGD EYLM UM TGVL TLVMLZLVRYKL. ~ MJLZL BEOM

23

42. JU FPRG XUZ VUEQ RTJ OZBBQOO FNVV LUVVUF. AROONUT NO GPQ LZQV DQPNTJ R OZBBQOOLZV BRIQQI. ~ HQK FPNGHRT

43. JOH NHGFHJ LS NEGGHNN RN JL ZL JOH GLWWLK JORKB EKGLWWLKVX THVV." ~ ILOK Z. FLGQHSHVVHF IF

44. GN GO ELN EUJUOODYC NL ZL USNYDLYZGEDYC NBGEFO NL FUN USNYDLYZGEDYC YUOHRNO." ~ MDYYUE WHVVUNN

45. LJGDFJ TDI SFJ S UJSMJF, RIBBJRR HR SLDIX YFDOHEY TDIFRJUG. OWJE TDI LJBDCJ S UJSMJF, RIBBJRR HR SLDIX YFDOHEY DXWJFR. ~ ZSBV OJUBW

---

46. PFCFGD, OWUEWZWUNGJW, NGR PWG TWNUE XM PUTFGD YFQQ WZWGPANQQT CNHW TXA QXXH QFHW NG XZWUGFDBP EAJJWEE. ~ IFL EPXGW

---

47. FUEC GIWNAC, FUEC DRRJOFG. ~ FUPSP XRTF

---

48. MUOYDDMJPQ MD YRPL IR YOMRMYR. ~ IRMC DMRVIP

---

49. VIVM FLZOMK C EOF-TOPV BZOWOW FR MRU FVIOCUV PZRE NRLZ KRCT. XOWURZN ZVEVEJVZW RMTN UXRWV QXR WLBBVVF. ~ XRBHWRM PTROM

---

50. Q CJKQYI NIBNSI HTB CYI DIYA LVUUILLEVS. GVO QE OTCO LVUUILL TCL GIIP CUTQIDIJ OTYBVRT OBB KVUT YVOTSILLPILL, OTIP Q KCA CJKQYI OTCO

NIYLBP, GVO Q UCP'O YILNIUO TQK. ~ YCOCP OCOC

---

51. UKCNKFN WU UWLLWFI WF LGN UGEJN LKJEM ZNPERUN UKCNKFN OSEFLNJ E LVNN E SKFI LWCN EIK. ~ TEVVNF ZRAANLL

---

52. D SGCGZ RZGXEGR XFJLW YLQQGYY. D OJZUGR BJZ DW. ~ GYWGG NXLRGZ

53. ZKQZUK QDJKW RGB JAGJ EQJSMGJSQW HQKRW'J UGRJ. PKUU, WKSJAKF HQKR YGJASWV — JAGJ'R PAB PK FKOQEEKWH SJ HGSUB. ~ TSV TSVUGF

---

54. R MUF CZ JWTTFJJ VM IKARDS ERJVFDFQ HFJGFTVPWEEZ VM VIF AFHZ OFJV KQARTF, KDQ VIFD SMRDS KUKZ KDQ QMRDS VIF FYKTV MGGMJRVF. ~ S.B. TIFJVFHVMD

28

55. AI TYP SCMJJT JYYZ DJYQCJT, XYQG YKCSUAEWG QPDDCQQCQ GYYZ M JYUE GAXC. ~ QGCKC VYHQ

---

56. WNJBJ MBJ OI EJHBJWE WI EDHHJEE. GW GE WNJ BJEDFW IC TBJTMBMWGIO, NMBP VIBL MOP FJMBOGOS CBIU CMGFDBJ. ~ HIFGO TIVJFF

---

57. CRXXKCC OC TDBKH EXLOKZKQ SI BLTCK NLT QTH'B MHTN BLEB DEOPRYK OC OHKZOBESPK. ~ XTXT XLEHKP

29

58. QIYNY'P LB PIBNQMSY BU NYOMNCMDKY VEYMP, FIMQ'P OVPPVLS VP QIY FVKK QB YZYRHQY QIYO. ~ PYQI SBEVL

59. A XHZ'V DZHU VNG UHLX 'PQAV.' GAVNGL A ZGSGL XAX, HL A NJSG JKHIACNGX AV. ~ CQCJZ KQVRNGL

60. APAB MZ FIV SKA IB DTA KMQTD DKSNO, FIV'HH QAD KVB IPAK MZ FIV UVED EMD DTAKA. ~ GMHH KIXQAKE

30

61. RKM UDHO CTO TXUZDS FA RKXUZVK. ~ XUIMXR GXUAR

62. XIUUCXX KX OVS SFC LCR SV FGHHKOCXX. FGHHKOCXX KX SFC LCR SV XIUUCXX. KY RVI MVNC ZFGS RVI GAC QVKOP, RVI ZKMM EC XIUUCXXYIM. ~ GMECAS XUFZCKSWCA

63. BMX UFA BK EXB LBFNBXC TL BK JHTB BFGYTZE FZC PXETZ CKTZE. ~ UFGB CTLZXA

64. MUVWUVD AZG WUBSO AZG HLS ZD MUVWUVD AZG WUBSO AZG HLS'W, AZG'DV DBKUW! – UVSDA JZDF

65. A DBBQ XNVX QKLM AC WEBWVEVXAIY GBBXAYF IWWIEXKYAXZ. ~ IWEVN SAYDEBZ

66. PDGGIPP RP QJC ARQFS; AFRSDLI RP QJC AFCFS: RC RP CWI GJDLFKI CJ GJQCRQDI CWFC GJDQCP. ~ URQPCJQ GWDLGWRSS

32

67. EUWTDL GXBL IHBLXVDB. EUWTDL EXHRSWDB. EUWTDL DZDWQLKHJT DPFDGL OKXL QUS'WD TUHJT LU CU JUO XJC CU HL. ~ OHRRHXI CSWXJL

68. UCYZ NP ILPT'K PCLIVFTK CFT STNSIT EWN BLB YND FTCILRT WNE AINKT DWTZ ETFT DN KVAATKK EWTY DWTZ XCQT VS. ~ DWNUCK TBLKNY

69. JSDYHBDD NTTNCLSHYLYBD UCB KYVB JSDBD, LEBCB'D UKPUZD UHNLEBC NHB FNIYHQ. ~ CYFEUCM JCUHDNH

70. QVFFLQQ VQVJNNC FMKLQ WM WGMQL XGM JEL WMM RVQC WM RL NMMTSUD HME SW. ~ GLUEC ZJYSZ WGMELJV

71. QBQN BS WZ RZ UZ ZHUMG UZ UOO BS WZ. ~ ENQ COUQTXUMY

72. XHPZ NZCFZHTAOU NOZT OR KPOFORK QXAZHT XQ TPWWZTT-OR ZRTPHORK XACX ZDZHBQRZ OT UZHMQHIORK CX XAZOH SZTX, FQORK XAZ YQHE XAZB CHZ

UNZFKZF XQ FQ CRF FQORK OX YZNN. ~ SONN QYZRT

---

73. DKAKRCDCAO UH SIUAR OQUARH BURQO; ECKSCBHQUY UH SIUAR OQC BURQO OQUARH. ~ YCOCB SBTNWCB

---

74. PNPDC YAFP CVG KBNP YV LHPBX, CVG BDP BGZAYAVUAUW IVD JPBZPDLKAH. ~ RBFPL KGFPL

---

75. FIY FB SCY SYQSQ FB VYWKYZQCAR AQ SCY WGAVASE SF ZYNFXIAHY W RZFGVYD GYBFZY AS GYNFDYQ WI YDYZXYINE. ~ WZIFVK XVWQFT

---

76. ILH KOCSUH XOSSHKI VQA IW OZJQYI QC WPSQCOFQIOWC OK IW EWYNK WC UHQMHPKLOJ MHGHUWJZHCI. ILHPH OK QUZWKI CW UOZOI IW ILH JWIHCIOQU WE QC WPSQCOFQIOWC ILQI PHYPNOIK SWWM JHWJUH, PQOKHK ILHZ NJ QK

UHQMHPK QCM YWCIOCNQUUA MHGHUWJK ILHZ. ~ RWLC ZQBVHUU

77. WLESIBHR M PLMVLF BQ QDHSHDISTQ UBGY WLESIBHR DSTFQLPK. BG BQ JFLEBQLPD GYMG QBIJPL MHV BG BQ MPQS GYMG VBKKBETPG. ~ UMFFLH WLHHBQ

78. IDS CHLQIGYL YC BSRUSOZDGX GZ IY XOYUHQS WYOS BSRUSOZ, LYI WYOS CYBBYESOZ. ~ ORBXD LRUSO

79. FDHNOD ENP UOD U JDUVDO, TPKKDTT WT UJJ UFNPS RONBWQR ENPOTDJH. BIDQ ENP FDKNLD U JDUVDO, TPKKDTT WT UJJ UFNPS RONBWQR NSIDOT. ~ XUKZ BDJKI

80. VC'L TVKS CQ ZSNSEYDCS LBZZSLL, EBC VC'L GQYS VGMQYCDKC CQ OSSH COS NSLLQKL QT TDVNBYS. ~ EVNN PDCSL

81. KNTS XZO LCSM JS CMTJ INJI XZO HOGI RJS'I GIZF INCSBCSU JDZOI, INJI'G

38

FYZDJDWX J UZZM ZST IZ FOYGOT. ~ HZGN HJVTG

---

82. ISRRGII MGQGJMI BJ GPQFBZGGI. OBV PG YJBUWJX EJM RBJJGRLWJX UWLD PZ GPQFBZGGI WI TGVZ WPQBVLEJL. ~ MWTWJG JMDFSYSFE

---

83. RWGS ZDRSHVMOX QSDQTS UWOH, MOPTFYMOX RWGMOX W PDRQWON HVWH QSDQTS UWOH HD UDJG KDJ. ~ ZWVMT TWLMOXMW

84. VS AZESZNFVBH PTTE. ZT WFOYSDNZP SKKTOD TO QTINFB WSENF VAGGMTOE IFZ VS F QAVQDNDADS KTO DCFD. ~ FZDCTZH JTBTEYNZ

85. MBSMZD BCCL UCE OTH UCCB PV OTH KHMB. PU ZCI KCV'O UPVK CVH, PO'D ZCI. ~ YMEL GIXMV

86. FV ESM DFGP SHCE YDSUP BPSBCP ESM MHRPGUYXHR, YDP QSWBXHE JFCC HPZPG IPY BPSBCP APYYPG YDXH ESM XGP.

40

XCJXEU GPWPWAPG YDXY ESM SVYPH VFHR SMYUYXHRFHI BPSBCP XWSHI YDSUP ESM RSH'Y BXGYFQMCXGCE CFOP. ~ USFQDFGS DSHRX

---

87. JA MEX QBAJLB MEXOCBTA FM PED MEX QJAABO AOEV RPB IEVSBRJRJEL, MEX'OB SOEFUFTM JL ROEXFTB. ~ EVUO PUVEXJ

---

88. PD TWN VNHJ AWFS WR HJNDD JMUJ TWN YPSQ URX TWN'FQ GUHHPWRUJQ UCWNJ, TWN XWR'J MULQ JW MULQ U

BUHJQF GYUR APJM MWA JMPREH APYY GYUT WNJ. ~ BUFS KNOSQFCQFE

89. MGMOZ NLWM XM CSIFAK S TMSNIOM, UMQUCM ZMCC SN IP. ~ SFDMCQ PQNLOS

90. NK RPIZUJKPIC – XPPM DPZ PLLPZFIGYFYKC FP LIF QPIZ BUGE IL UGE BUSK U JP. NURM QPIZCKXD. ~ JUYX MKXXQ

91. OXNYT FXT PCYCLJ, JLF FXT VLJTZ, FXT VLJTZ RCMM TJG BQ KLMMLRCJI ZLB. ~ FLJZ XYCTX

92. AWLU FWJS LGTNKKA XLJSWFIUJ NUI AWLU OUINSIJS JWLUXI WB EINUGRGO. ~ PREE ONSIJ

93. DSWN NZNXU QNASTF YNXINOA SEQ FTDTA ALN ERDHNX PI QNASTFJ AP YNXINOA." ~ CSOW QPXJNU

94. CMXYX HL UD FYXECXY CMHUF SDP JEU ZD KHCM SDPY AHTX EUZ SDPY KDYN CMEU TDAADK SDPY QELLHDUL - HU E KES CMEC LXYBXL CMX KDYAZ EUZ SDP. ~ YHJMEYZ WYEULDU

---

95. WJS NDZJ RO UDL RN XRYO UCIOSJUS NODJTQU DT I ORRC ITQ IUP SKJC SR OISJ XRYO DQJI. ~ CIOP BDTMYU

---

96. XWIC DUQTWXDDM GWUD VRCMK. EOA RV XWI KCDEK XWIC DUQTWXDDM CRSLK,

44

SIDMM PLEK? XWIC GIMKWUDCM GWUD HEGF, EOA KLEK UEFDM XWIC MLECDLWTADCM LEQQX. MKECK PRKL DUQTWXDDM EOA KLD CDMK VWTTWPM VCWU KLEK. ~ LDCH FDTTDLDC

---

97. AP BZH RFQ DZI QSCRFFRGGQX CB ILQ PAFGI UQFGAZD ZP BZHF TFZXHNI, BZH'UQ MRHDNLQX IZZ MRIQ. ~ FQAX LZPPSRD

98. EJMI GWLF WA DWLWGFN, AJ NJH'G RQAGF WG DWXWHV AJLFJHF FDAF'A DWPF. ~ AGFXF BJCA

99. CJDCKQ SYJEGYZ FVZY ONCB YPLYHOYS. ~ JCZZK LCUY

100. XMRA KQ EQT FGGK AQ CARJA R LTCDFGCC? AMJGG CDPBHG AMDFVC: ZFQX EQTJ BJQKTIA LGAAGJ AMRF RFEQFG, ZFQX EQTJ ITCAQPGJ, RFK MRSG R LTJFDFV KGCDJG AQ CTIIGGK. ~ KRSG AMQPRC

101. IBKIZE SNWYO CTSEWMU SNU VCA IYM UGVFIXU CQQCFSTYWSWUE SNIS IQQUIF, KNUFUHUF SNUZ GWPNS VU. ~ BIOENGW GWSSIB

102. PKW RBP XJBKWIO, QD ODJ HDT'W WBN DYY NDWKTWBMI VDLNKWBWDEQ. ~ VGEBQ HBUDT

103. IE JCIXPW ITC OEFXOIF EH ITEMC STE XJC BJCMCWI, RC OEFXO IE ITEMC STE XJC XRMCWI. ~ MICBTCW J. DEKCF

104.   LJECLFCLJLMC YH HDPLDJL AQD QKH K GYHYDJ UDC HDPLEQYJX KJW K AKJE ED NCLKEL. ~ WKGYW BKCF

105.   GW JAP PWL, Y MGRGQW BGJAQTJ JAP YKGHGJU JQ PVPDTJP GJ GR SOQKYKHU Y AYHHTDGWYJGQW. ~ RJPMP DYRP

106.   UBFSAUQ TSIQVUPW MGJ QUMPDCU KRU DBFSQKMGHU SW HSGKQDNIKDGE KS KRU ASQPJ NT PDYDGE TSIQ KMPUGK. ASQX SG ARMK TSI PSYU. TSI MQU

QUVFSGVDNPU WSQ KRU KMPUGK KRMK RMV NUUG UGKQIVKUJ KS TSI. ~ HMKRMQDGM NQIGV

---

107.   UA'D YCA HPCWA UIJHD. UA'D HPCWA RHVUYE UIJHD NHKKJY. ~ DXCAA PJSDVB

---

108.   G IHV'C JHHQ CH TDFB HZYS 7-EHHC WKSP — G JHHQ EHS 1-EHHC WKSP CLKC G UKV PCYB HZYS. ~ OKSSYV WDEEYCC

109. EPK HOFBMEYCE EPHCT HX CBE IKHCT YUMYHR EB EYQK Y NPYCNK. MKOKOIKM, EPK TMKYEKXE UYHGLMK HX EB CBE EMA. BCNK ABL UHCR XBOKEPHCT ABL GBZK EB RB, IK EPK IKXE YE RBHCT HE. ~ RKIIH UHKGRX

110. FQE'D CLD QDNLZB TQEHUETL AQX DNPD DNL UFLP UB SQQF ONLE AQXZ SXD DLCCB AQX UD'B WPF. ~ RLHUE ZQBL

50

111. YXYZINCKHU TNBZNYS BT HJNCKHU.

~ FYH EYKTTYHTNYKH

---

112. TLRD QGTI JYHS GJYITR JYLSD LR RHKI. BTIHQ QGTI JYHS GJYITR JYLSD LR VTHPJLPHU. ~ YGZHTB RPYAUJW

---

113. NSH'J OI DATDPN JS DYYITJ ESZTYIVA, CDKI WSHAPNIHWI PH ESZT DOPVPJPIY DHN NSH'J VIJ JCI ODYJDTNY RIJ ESZ NSLH.

~ XPWCDIV OVSSXOITR

114. CTD'R YUGUR STKALJYP. GFDS MJTMYJ YUGUR RVJGLJYBJL RT OVFR RVJS RVUDQ RVJS HFD CT. STK HFD ET FL PFA FL STKA GUDC YJRL STK. OVFR STK IJYUJBJ, AJGJGIJA, STK HFD FHVUJBJ. ~ GFAS QFS FLV

---

115. ZHV YDWB EH GBB SDKUVFB DG EYB OBTKXXKXT DXM EYB CKMMUB, OVE XBWBF BXEBFEDKX KE DG DX BXM. ~ QBGGKJD YBFFKX

116. GMP BJKW GMSJV RBTFP GMXJ FGXTGSJV FBIPGMSJV XJZ UXSKSJV... SF JBG FGXTGSJV FBIPGMSJV. ~ FPGM VBZSJ

117. OPJW QSA HLJ UACVTCWN H GFHLFAE, CF'G TCYYCKAVF. EHLFCKAVHLVQ, H GFHLFAE FPHF CG JBEHWTCWN HF FPJ LHFJ SY FCWTJL. QSA PHRJ FS NCRJ 100%, HWT QSA PHRJ FS UJ KSXXCFFJT. GSVRCWN FPJ ELSUVJX PHG FS UJ EJLGSWHV SL JVGJ QSA'LJ NSCWN FS TCGCWFJNLHFJ. ~ GJHW LHT

53

118. CT QI LMCIH LB LUCAS BT K XBBH CHIK, QI QBPGHA'L UKZI VIIA KVGI LB LUCAS BT K XBBH CHIK. WBP NPRL UKZI LB TCAH LUI RBGPLCBA TBM K EMBVGIY CA WBPM BQA GCTI. ~ VMCKA JUIRSW

119. N IUAACP KNJL TCY PQL XCVWYMU XCV HYIILHH, OYP N IUA KNJL TCY PQL XCVWYMU XCV XUNMYVL, SQNIQ NH: PVT PC DMLUHL LJLVTOCGT. ~ QLVOLVP HSCDL

120. POQYQGVSHVR ICGSCKY RP POQ PB QUCHK LGA QP WPPYQ QUC YCIB-CYQCCD PB QUCHK ZCKYPVVCI. HB ZCPZIC WCIHCNC HV QUCDYCINCY, HQ'Y GDGTHVR LUGQ QUCA FGV GFFPDZIHYU. ~ YGD LGIQPV

121. JE MDCQ NRZJDXO JXOTJQI DZFIQO ZD WQINV VDQI, GINQX VDQI, WD VDQI NXW YIRDVI VDQI, MDC NQI N GINWIQ. ~ ADFX SCJXRM NWNVO

122. QDNJY SNJMNDT JDN XRSSRFQ YI TJBDRWRBN YON FPLANDT YI TJUN YON HNIHSN. HIID SNJMNDT TJBDRWRBN YON HNIHSN YI TJUN YON FPLANDT. ~ TRLIF TRFNG

---

123. UBFBKVUVFQ OX GJSLXOFK JF KVQQOFK XJUVJFV QJ KVQ B CVXLDQ. DVBIVCXNOZ OX ZCJILSOFK B XQBFIBCI OF XJUVJFV QNBQ YNVF TJL'CV KJFV, QNVT YODD DOAV WT QJ ZCJILSV NOKNVC

DVAVD CVXLDQX SJFXOXQVFQDT. ~ QJFT CJWWOFX

124. ILVZLEPRYS ZXLP BXN VIJVWP JLVE NRL RVEBLPP XG HXDSEXDYPL. ~ JXXZEXJ JYIPXB

125. GAYRAFPMCL CP HMA OYLYOCHB HE HFYVPGYHA ICPCEV CVHE FAYGCHB. ~ SYFFAV UAVVCP

126. XDG'Z JHGX JCTPZ, JHGX C FMNMXL. ~ YMGFL JDFX

127. UDXEDZLQOF OL CPBTOPH TQDP GB UDXP BP BGQDZL XPE UDG GQDY LGDF RF XPE LQOPD. ~ YOWQDUUD FDURLB

128. EHHEIB HDIW IHTBA WHR ZKBD BTBSWHDB BIAB IHTBA WHR VNSAY. ~ ZBDCW FNBSALII

129. XB WTLK HTZESZE XIZ'E RKXDXZN HTZDSKIFEXTZ, WTL'KS RTXZN XE PKTZN. ~ RFZ KTEV

---

130. VLKZTKZ OD QOKM RNZ TKMFMTSTKZ OD GNTTK, FKI ZPT CFIA HNCTD ZPT PLNDT! ~ SFHO DSOZP

---

131. ZU TEL HLZPW ZI ... TEL OJT GIZPP XDDW QEEQPD JWYEBWG. ~ NDXXZUDB ODGDXHBZXM

132. SU VWL TOB'A IDCKOSB SA AW O 6-VIOP-WKY, VWL YWB'A JBWH SA VWLPRIKU. ~ OKFIPA ISBRAISB

133. QVANCQU UJHIA RIB HDHJ ILNCHDHK RCANVXA HQANXBCIBY. ~ JIFON RIFKV HYHJBVQ

134. BCKYP OKR UYL LJY'B FKDBNY BJ INJIFN TCJ BNFF ZJA KB WUY'B ON LJYN. FKGN'D BJJ DCJMB BJ BCKYP DHUFF. ~ BKH GNMMKDD

60

135. VUKZLCB KN NKIHZA PDB THHTCPLRKPA PT JBFKR UFUKR, PDKN PKIB ITCB KRPBZZKFBRPZA. ~ DBRCA VTCE

136. AQ ZMF BMV'N JOSX UMMP NM QOAD, ZMF BMV'N JOSX UMMP NM KUMT. ~ GMVONJOV PADBXVJODD

137. SQ GKTHNDSRJ SG STFKPNXRN HRKVJD, HZHR SQ NDH KEEG XPH XJXSRGN AKV, AKV GDKVIE GNSII EK SN. ~ HIKR TVGU

138. PQXF IDPB LSOE DLSBPX LSQEF QX XOJB. VPBOI IDPB LSOE DLSBPX LSQEF QX CPOWLQWOY. ~ SDGOPV XWSNYLA

139. OK'C ZXCA KT NTYZ GM QOKV IZQ OBZXC; KVZ VXPB MXPK OC DZKKOIJ JT TH QVXK QTPUZB HTP ATG KQT AZXPC XJT, WGK QODD CTTI WZ TGK TH BXKZ. ~ PTJZP STI TZNV

140. BTOCDJI ON TZMUPIJ NUIGGOZL NUMZI UM LJITUZINN. ~ MGJTP ROZBJIV

141. QYAI BWWPWAGM, XYW QYAI BTWPWAGM, DPJJ GMWMICPXM QYAI BJWPWAGM. ~ LPV LPVJBI

142. GTV EVMG JQW GP HUVCSRG GTV AYGYUV SM GP RUVQGV SG. ~ HVGVU CUYRDVU

143. OYLDFGCGFA GN GBFLJJGKLBOL PDCGBK XEB. ~ DJQLYF LGBNFLGB

144. SJTRA RKT TRAI. SHBOTHTDGRGSED SA URKJ. ~ FQI NRXRARNS

145. FGPKEDHDEB, KT QKT APPW TKDO, FMWTDTET CKGSPCB MN GPKGGKWSDWS ZQKE ZP UWMZ DW MGOPG EM NDWO MVE ZQKE ZP OM WME UWMZ. QPWFP, EM EQDWU FGPKEDHPCB, ZP RVTE AP KACP EM CMMU KNGPTQ KE ZQKE ZP WMGRKCCB EKUP NMG SGKWEPO. ~ SPMGSP UWPCCPG

146. OI THHTIAJON OHXTBA SQ BDTOAJMJAE JH ISA GTJIZ OQDOJP AS QOJN." ~ TPVJI NOIP

147. ISSJ EBYPRVLQI EBPRD VKR TSEOBQZ WSSP DEBYV. IYRBV EBYPRVLQI EBPRD VKR TXDVSERY HRRW DEBYV. ~ ASR TKRYQSU

148. RZOBZOK X2X JK X2E, L XOGLOWO QDHHLJADBOGN BZDB TJJV IDKMOBLAT OHHOABLDGH DKO BZO HDIO. RO DGG

DKO OIJBLJADG XOLATH GJJMLAT SJK KOGOWDAEO, EJABOUB DAV EJAAOEBLJA. ~ XOBZ EJIHBJEM

---

149. QDVUOSFIM FL IK HKIMOV DJKRS SCO LSRWW SCDS TKR QDUO, JRS DJKRS SCO LSKVFOL TKR SOHH. ~ LOSC MKPFI

---

150. LVCPFXKUW KZ CFVMMB NOZX VJHOX ZTVCKUW BHOC AVZZKHU. ~ LKQTVFM TBVXX

66

151. VDQ VS PYQ KQHP OLMH PV HLKVPLWQ MVAZ TVDPQDP RH PV DVP PRQ RP PV MVAZ WVLBH. CDVO OYM MVA'ZQ TZQLPRDW TVDPQDP. ~ QBBQD WVGQH

---

152. HV ZSO'DY T QSSB LTDGYUHPQ NYDWSP, ZSO KTJY US CY T FHUUFY EDTXZ. ~ RHL LYUETFV

---

153. NMKOFAWXU WD AFRRWXU ASF IGKRT HGP'KF M KGQO DAMK. QGXAFXA

NMKOFAWXU WD DSGIWXU ASF IGKRT HGP MKF GXF. ~ KGYFKA KGDF

---

154. UXXQ HKFNPWPFT TPP MXGTEHPFT KT MXHBDPWP LEHKG JPCGUT YCWL KDD WLP QCHPGTCXGT FPKD BPXBDP LKAP." ~ RXGKL TKMLT

---

155. BLIE BUNNFHQ. BLPZL RUNEFHQ. ~ JFQ JFQNPZ

156. TADU GHL ENG MW, MW'E ZNJVDWMUF. TADU WADG ENG MW, MW'E EHSMNI QJHHO. ~ NUKG SJDEWHKMUN

157. OSHMU HN, EGU NRBZ XHMM DWIB; WGMZ XWKTJ HG NRB IWQHBJ. JWDHEM IBUHE HJ E OSHMU HN, GSKNSKB HN, BGVEVB NRBI EGU NRBZ IEZ DWIB EGU JNEZ. ~ JBNR VWUHG

158. NIPBQD VOXBQ BN QRIAY YCO FOIFDO. KIY QRIAY JIAW RANBKONN.

FWIEBXO TIW YCO FOIFDO QKX YCO FOIFDO ZBDD FWIEBXO TIW JIA. ~ VQYY LIADQWY

---

159. RMFCWP ZDTCW CR W FMHQWFQ RSMAQ. ~ ZWAEWADQ ZMPPMK

---

160. FJNPEFNB AVDL YFKZ, SVK'N RDZN JVOOBJN NCBW OPGB XFZBXFOO JFLSZ. ~ RFA XFBL

---

161. S DMSTG YI TE OETXRM CVSF CR FROO FVR PETIJWRM YF YI — YF YI CVSF PETIJWRMI FROO RSPV EFVRM YF YI." ~ IPEFF PEEH

162. YDXKSZ BFNYKEWE DSL XWWBKSZ QJWY KE D ZFWDQ GDA QN VRKCL D VFDSL. ~ EWQJ ZNLKS

163. BQFJ NJLPY ZG L GOQJB FPCQAYZPR LMJQGG LAA MFGOQIVJ OQFMTEQZPOG. ~ KQPLT GLMTG

164. XN AWY'DT PWH NKXOXPR PWL KPB KRKXP, XH'V K VXRP AWY'DT PWH BWXPR KPAHJXPR XPPWFKHXFT." ~ LWWBA KOOTP

---

165. GY ITM'JX ATO ZOMVVTJA, ITM'KK EGHX ML TA XSLXJGUXAOZ OTT ZTTA. QAF GY ITM'JX ATO YKXSGVKX, ITM'KK LTMAF ITMJ DXQF QEQGAZO ODX PQKK QAF ITM PTA'O ZXX Q FGYYXJXAO ZTKMOGTA OT Q LJTVKXU ITM'JX OJIGAE OT ZTKHX. ~ RXYY VXBTZ

166. X'O PWLQNP WJMEMVXIN LQWD LM KN ZM LXCXO WZ LM DNSNP LPR LM OM WDRLQXDV ZCWPL MP KPWSN. ~ ENN UEMA

---

167. FB ZQG'YO WQQCFVL BQY RTO VOKR UFL RTFVL, MVS ZQG'YO WQQCFVL DTOYO OIOYZQVO OWHO FH, ZQG'YO WQQCFVL FV RTO DYQVL AWMNO. ~ PMYC NGUMV

168. MH ANW LN DUYJ ANW'RF YKDYAC LNZF, ANW'KK BFJ DUYJ ANW'RF YKDYAC BNJJFZ. ~ JNZA SNVVMZC

---

169. EVX HWVUC UTV CPAVMHAVC SPOEW HE MRV APCM JTUEODUT WVMUHDC PS U GTPKDVA XRVTV SVX PMRVTC KPMRVT MP DPPY. ~ EUMV CHDIVT

---

170. VN ACQO XRLVCMD VMDJVOB CLSBOD LC TOBXU UCOB, KBXOM UCOB, TC UCOB

74

XMT ZBRCUB UCOB, ACQ'OB X KBXTBO. ~ FCSM EQVMRA XTXUD

171. XSFAXDVEXIS KINFS'E DNFAISK EI RNNEXSU DNJPNFEF. CIP ZVS'E FZQNKPON UDNVESNFF. ~ TVC LVND

172. OX UG HDDW OAGOP YJRD RAG JGMR FGJRKBZ, HGOPGBX UYHH NG RADXG UAD GTQDUGB DRAGBX. ~ NYHH EORGX

173. OKB RWBIOBNO HBIVBW SN YDO YBUBNNIWSHA OKB DYB FKD VDBN OKB RWBIOBNO OKSYRN. KB SN OKB DYB OKIO RBON OKB TBDTHB OD VD OKB RWBIOBNO OKSYRN. ~ WDYIHV WBIRIY

174. XJ SJM VJRRJI INCZC MNC AQMN OQB RCQX. UJ YSEMCQX INCZC MNCZC YE SJ AQMN QSX RCQKC Q MZQYR. ~ ZQRAN IQRXJ COCZEJS

175. AJR QRBU RKKRLPR GV NRMFRBKJWH WK AJMA UGD JMQR AG JMQR QWKWGL. UGD PML'A ENGO ML DLPRBAMWL ABDIHRA. ~ AJRGFGBR I. JRKEDBTJ

---

176. PEPQI LOZSY UOL O AOLY... PEPQI LZSSPQ UOL O GJYJQP. ~ HLNOQ TZRMP

---

177. BQW JWOOMSMOB PRSJNGMFO GHRAB BQW TMFY. BQW RJBMSMOB WLJWPBO MB BR PQGFCW. BQW NWGYWI GYVAOBO BQW OGMNO. ~ VRQF SGLTWNN

77

178. G FIIE IWSVXHQLV ID TVGEVJNCQR QN HI CVTR HCINV YCI GJV EIQPF RIIJTK HI EI YVTT GPE HI CVTR HCINV YCI GJV EIQPF YVTT HI EI VLVP WVHHVJ. ~ SQZ JICP

---

179. XDN QUBN UI OUMX BNCRNQM TM XU ANX XDN FNUFBN XU XDTSJ OUQN UI XDN BNCRNQ KGX XDN QUBN UI XDN NHWNFXTUSCB BNCRNQ TM XU ANX XDN FNUFBN XU XDTSJ OUQN UI XDNOMNBPNM. ~ KUUJNQ X. VCMDTSAXUS

78

180. WEH'O YLU XEK TJIIRTT LX AEJ DYHO LO; PJTO WE DCYO AEJ QESR YHW MRQLRSR LH, YHW LO DLQQ IEUR HYOJKYQQA. ~ WYSLW XKETO

181. BJ SOKBJNKK, KOLLNKKCOY ENXEYN INWLG PXWYK, JXQ HOXQWK. ~ KQNEGNJ RNIDUJ

182. ZCNMBJK NQ SPK GYFLNXKFS SPCS WNOKQ QBGGKQQ NS'Q ZMCOYJ. ~ SJBXCF GCIYSK

183. GHOOXGG KG EUA AQX DXF AU QRIIKEXGG. QRIIKEXGG KG AQX DXF AU GHOOXGG. KB FUH MUSX NQRA FUH RYX TUKEW, FUH NKMM JX GHOOXGGBHM. ~ QXYLRE ORKE

184. ABI NTVNAR FNRR WNKTICU BD ABIC VNA GB RIYYURR. ~ SKYQUA CBBDUA

185. MJR CRGM HRKRQPR TG FBGGTKR GXIIRGG. ~ EHBQA GTQBMHB

186. GZCETZ EC PKZ FZN PB RBPEXVPEBL, QAP EP'C GZPZTRELVPEBL VLG DBRREPRZLP PB VL ALTZSZLPELO MATCAEP BJ NBAT OBVS - V DBRREPRZLP PB ZHDZSSZLDZ - PKVP IESS ZLVQSZ NBA PB VPPVEL PKZ CADDZCC NBA CZZF. ~ RVTEB VLGTZPPE

---

187. YAIEUWMH CO YPA ITCVCYX YW UWMH YWQAYPAM YWUIMK I BWEEWD SCOCWD. YPA ITCVCYX YW KCMABY CDKCSCKGIV IBBWEJVCOPEADYO YWUIMK

WMQIDCRIYCWDIV WTFABYCSAO. CY CO YPA LGAV YPIY IVVWUO BWEEWD JAWJVA YW IYYICD GDBWEEWD MAOGVYO. ~ IDKMAU BIMDAQCA

---

188. FCTQV H VMCHP PCHUUHPC TD YRMG, JHMN YRMG. TP MCSATMCD TQPCQPTRQ HQN NTDLTIKTQC, EADP KTGC FCLRUTQV H FCPPCM JTPPCM RM H FCPPCM DHKCDICMDRQ. FAP TP TD H DGTKK DCP PJHP T FCKTCWC RPJCMD, KTGC UC, LHQ KCHMQ. ~ NHWTN MRDD

189.   VK'H USK QISNK PSFLVUJ OQFC, VK'H QISNK PSFLVUJ KSJYKOYF. BSN OQAY KS MQFY ESFY QISNK KOY KYQE KOQU BSN CS QISNK BSNFHYXD. ~ GSOU MQXVRQFV

---

190.   K'V Y QWUUJQQ ATRYC ZJUYWQJ K GYR Y HPKJDR IGT ZJBKJFJR KD VJ YDR K RKRD'A GYFJ AGJ GJYPA AT BJA GKV RTID. ~ YZPYGYV BKDUTBD

---

191.   BUM QLP AUI VU TS WTQR CRFRSCE US AUIP XRTSV HRSCRP MTHB HBR AUISV,

KUJFLEETUSLHR MTHB HBR LVRC, EAJFLHBRHTK MTHB HBR EHPTGTSV LSC HUWRPLSH UQ HBR MRLO LSC EHPUSV. XRKLIER EUJRCLA TS AUIP WTQR AUI MTWW BLGR XRRS LWW UQ HBRER. ~ VRUPVR MLEBTSVHUS KLPGRP

192. W BIYWBIB D KTXM NWOI DMT NCDN WP W HDF MTWXM NT CTKB MJGBMIF WX EGFWXIFF, WN HTGKB NGJX WXNT D PGKK-NWOI ZTE. ~ KDQIKK IBHDJBF

193. KSXUXNR XF QVKN RTZ'MG DKHKSUG TE OTXJW. BTNXLKNXTJ OGNGMBXJGF QVKN RTZ OT. KNNXNZOG OGNGMBXJGF VTQ QGUU RTZ OT XN. ~ UTZ VTUNY

194. OFWX F QZXLUX LXTYCWX ZI XWXLSDOZIA SYJ MY. MXRYITDLFDX MXDXLRZIFDZYI, LXTZCZXIUS, FIM DXIFUZDS. MY IYD CXD DXRGYLFLS TXDVFUET VXUYRX GXLRFIXID XHUJTXT. JTX RZTDFEXT FIM GLYVCXRT FT

85

YGGYLDJIZDZXT DY AXD VXDDXL-IYD LXFTYIT DY NJZD. ~ KFRZX MZRYI

195. AB PXB LEXXCEHKBK BQBXU KPU OU FBCFDB AIC KC YIPHSDBLL OEY JRFCXYPHY ACXS. ~ OXJPH SJDRBPKB

196. THDEHVJHUX HD FBX BHCBXDF WISY IW JIOX. HW AIN SXGJJA JIOX DIYXIUX, AIN BGOX FI CHOX FBXY FBX JXOXJ IW THDEHVJHUX FBXA UXXT. ~ FIY HPPI

197. EXB XIKJBGE XIWPE EY JBCBHYL PG EY VPS. EXB LBYLHB VXY JBCBHYL EXPG

XIWPE SBCBK EIRB VPSSPSA UYK AKISEBJ,
EXBO SBCBK UBBH BSEPEHBJ EY CPTEYKO.
~ FPRB RKDODBVGRP

---

198. HX PT KVAYZ PBMV HK JTCTRZ MGTCMWT, PT PHRR CTJMHE JTCTRZ MGTCMWT. ~ KBMPE MOBNC

---

199. I JURRCG UW WVOCVRC JDV PIR SVVE UR KDC OUGGVG IK KDC CRF VL KDC FIZ IRF WIZ UR XMGWMUK VL OZ YVIS IRF FGCIOW U YINC OZ QCWK. ~ FUPE NUKISC

200. SRSQX LHX GS DHRS HA VZZVQPTANPX PV WQSHPS H CNRNAI OHJPSQZNSWS. ~ ONWDHSC ISQRHNJ

201. QRPZ CJQDW NJQ THOW CQ GHBP SOWHCPZ XHR WEWO HXJBWEW SOWHCPZ. ~ OQMWOC G. VWRRWTZ

202. T UKTGDIQH LDTKG XV T JDUXEEXEU FI UKDTGEDVV. XG XV TE DZYKDVVXFE FI LQNXHXGA. XG XV T IFQESTGXFE IFK GLD SDMDHFYNDEG FI VQPL MXKGQDV TV YKTADK, ITXGL, PFQKTUD, PFEGDEGNDEG,

88

LTYYXEDVV, HFMD, TES RDHH-JDXEU. ~ WTNDV D. ITQVG

203. QV SCK GIOGAE CI ROVGKSVJJ. JCWV GOV QCOS ROVGK, JCWV GNYAVMV ROVGKSVJJ, GSE CKYVOJ YGMV ROVGKSVJJ KYOBJK BTCS KYVW. ~ FAZZAGW JYGXVJTVGOV

204. QII WBGGVOVIVEVNG QTN BR ELN BELNT GVHN BS ZNG. ZBP LQUN EB LQUN Q ZNG AVRHGNE EB MNE EB MTNQERNGG. ~ KBLR X. AQCYNII

205. DUHB ZAP'WH LAAC XI VAOHIUEBL, ZAP'YY IHYY HGHWZABH. DUHB ZAP'WH LWHXI XI VAOHIUEBL, IUHZ'YY IHYY ZAP. ~ DXYIHW RXZIAB

206. ECCJ PDPZ MTXI JCXJSC DKX OTZ OX YCSFOOSC ZXVT PIYFOFXQB. BIPSS JCXJSC PSDPZB OTZ OX UX OKPO, YVO OKC TCPSSZ WTCPO IPEC ZXV MCCS OKPO ZXV, OXX, PTC WTCPO. ~ IPTE ODPFQ

HINTS

Your Hints :

Your First Hints :

1.	T = E
2.	Q = I
3.	B = L
4.	P = E
5.	P = M
6.	H = N
7.	G = W
8.	J = Q
9.	A = W
10.	Y = B
11.	E = M
12.	I = M
13.	C = D
14.	H = S
15.	L = V
16.	H = J
17.	Y = O
18.	U = K
19.	X = Y
20.	E = D
21.	A = F
22.	H = P
23.	K = G
24.	L = B
25.	E = D
26.	L = N

Your Second Hints :

1.	E = A
2.	K = E
3.	P = A
4.	E = A
5.	S = O
6.	J = E
7.	V = O
8.	P = E
9.	D = E
10.	M = A
11.	V = O
12.	A = I
13.	X = E
14.	K = R
15.	C = E
16.	J = A
17.	U = I
18.	T = I
19.	H = E
20.	J = A
21.	C = E
22.	Q = E
23.	X = E
24.	Z = T
25.	Q = O
26.	N = A

27. G = O
28. J = O
29. D = Y
30. G = E
31. K = H
32. O = E
33. I = R
34. U = H
35. H = P
36. X = A
37. W = P
38. J = W
39. X = G
40. Q = Y
41. V = R
42. I = R
43. E = U
44. Z = D
45. R = S
46. G = N
47. P = E
48. M = I
49. B = C
50. U = C
51. E = A
52. B = F
53. V = G
54. B = K
55. X = M
56. U = M

27. Q = T
28. X = I
29. M = O
30. N = U
31. W = E
32. D = O
33. W = O
34. Y = E
35. X = T
36. I = Y
37. X = S
38. W = A
39. H = I
40. P = E
41. Y = N
42. U = O
43. L = O
44. U = E
45. S = A
46. W = E
47. F = S
48. D = S
49. R = O
50. Q = I
51. U = S
52. D = I
53. Q = O
54. J = S
55. Y = O
56. M = A

57. K = E	57. C = S
58. O = M	58. P = S
59. L = R	59. I = A
60. E = S	60. M = I
61. R = T	61. U = O
62. P = G	62. X = S
63. K = O	63. F = A
64. U = H	64. V = E
65. W = P	65. A = I
66. A = F	66. P = S
67. P = X	67. U = O
68. A = C	68. C = A
69. S = U	69. N = O
70. H = F	70. V = U
71. W = U	71. B = O
72. C = A	72. Z = E
73. K = A	73. U = I
74. J = L	74. P = E
75. T = W	75. F = O
76. B = X	76. H = E
77. I = M	77. L = E
78. O = R	78. S = E
79. P = U	79. D = E
80. H = D	80. V = I
81. H = J	81. T = E
82. G = E	82. I = S
83. U = W	83. S = E
84. K = F	84. S = E
85. Y = M	85. M = A
86. X = A	86. F = I

87. X = U	87. J = I
88. N = U	88. W = O
89. P = S	89. Z = Y
90. I = U	90. K = E
91. J = N	91. F = T
92. G = N	92. A = Y
93. J = S	93. N = E
94. X = E	94. U = I
95. D = I	95. J = E
96. D = E	96. D = E
97. F = R	97. B = Y
98. M = U	98. F = E
99. H = C	99. C = A
100. J = R	100. R = A
101. W = I	101. I = A
102. L = M	102. K = E
103. M = S	103. C = E
104. B = K	104. Y = I
105. U = Y	105. G = I
106. B = M	106. U = E
107. H = A	107. U = I
108. Q = K	108. H = O
109. A = Y	109. E = T
110. O = W	110. Q = O
111. F = B	111. T = S
112. Y = H	112. L = I
113. N = D	113. S = O
114. P = F	114. U = I
115. M = D	115. D = A
116. P = E	116. P = E

117. P = H	
118. S = K	
119. Y = U	
120. R = G	
121. X = N	
122. J = A	
123. W = B	
124. E = R	
125. B = Y	
126. D = O	
127. E = D	
128. I = L	
129. B = F	
130. G = Q	
131. N = J	
132. W = O	
133. C = I	
134. A = U	
135. L = U	
136. M = O	
137. A = Y	
138. D = O	
139. T = O	
140. U = T	
141. I = R	
142. V = E	
143. Y = R	
144. K = R	
145. U = K	
146. S = O	

117. J = E	
118. C = I	
119. A = N	
120. G = A	
121. J = I	
122. Q = G	
123. B = A	
124. V = A	
125. E = O	
126. M = E	
127. U = L	
128. H = O	
129. X = I	
130. V = C	
131. Z = I	
132. I = S	
133. I = A	
134. K = I	
135. U = A	
136. M = O	
137. K = O	
138. Q = I	
139. C = S	
140. T = A	
141. Y = O	
142. G = T	
143. J = L	
144. R = A	
145. P = E	
146. O = A	

147. H = F
148. V = D
149. P = D
150. N = J
151. B = L
152. U = T
153. N = M
154. N = K
155. E = P
156. U = N
157. B = E
158. W = R
159. H = N
160. Y = F
161. I = S
162. L = D
163. A = L
164. Y = U
165. V = B
166. A = W
167. P = M
168. A = Y
169. O = U
170. D = S
171. R = M
172. D = O
173. S = I
174. X = D
175. I = M
176. H = O

147. S = O
148. X = B
149. D = A
150. V = A
151. V = O
152. H = I
153. M = A
154. X = O
155. B = S
156. D = E
157. O = B
158. N = S
159. W = A
160. F = A
161. S = A
162. D = A
163. Q = O
164. X = I
165. X = E
166. X = I
167. O = E
168. N = O
169. V = E
170. C = O
171. I = O
172. O = A
173. B = E
174. J = O
175. R = E
176. P = E

177. C = G
178. F = G
179. W = C
180. A = Y
181. Q = T
182. C = A
183. Y = R
184. D = N
185. C = B
186. X = V
187. C = I
188. J = H
189. V = I
190. C = Y
191. W = L
192. B = D
193. F = S
194. Q = F
195. F = P
196. C = G
197. P = I
198. J = M
199. U = I
200. D = H
201. J = H
202. G = T
203. R = G
204. B = O
205. B = N
206. J = P

177. W = E
178. G = A
179. N = E
180. W = O
181. B = I
182. N = I
183. H = U
184. B = O
185. R = E
186. Z = E
187. I = A
188. F = B
189. S = O
190. K = I
191. U = O
192. W = I
193. K = A
194. F = A
195. B = E
196. H = I
197. B = E
198. T = E
199. I = A
200. S = E
201. Q = O
202. T = A
203. Q = B
204. I = L
205. H = E
206. C = E

SOLUTIONS

1. If people are doubting how far you'll go, go so far that you can't hear them anymore. – Michele Ruiz

2. Thinking is the hardest work there is, which is probably the reason so few engage in it. ~ Henry Ford

3. Satisfaction lies in the effort, not in the attainment. ~ *Mahatma Gandhi*

4. Hard work beats talent if talent doesn't work hard. ~ *Tim Notke*

5. No matter how hard you work, someone else is working harder. ~ *Elon Musk*

6. I'm a great believer in luck, and I find the harder I work, the more I have of it. ~ *Thomas Jefferson*

7. A dream does not become reality through magic; it takes sweat, determination, and hard work. ~ *Colin Powell*

8. We think, mistakenly, that success is the result of the amount of time we put in at work, instead of the quality of time we put in. ~ *Ariana Huffington*

9. Men die of boredom, psychological conflict and disease. They do not die of hard work. ~ *David Ogilvy*

10. The only place where success comes before work is in the dictionary. ~ *Vidal Sassoon*

11. Work hard, have fun, make history. ~ *Jeff Bezos*

12. I never took a day off in my 20s. Not one. ~ *Bill Gates*

13. There are no secrets to success. It is the result of preparation, hard work, and learning from failure. ~ *Colin Powell*

14. Without labor, nothing prospers. ~ *Sophocles*

15. There is no time for cut-and-dried monotony. There is time for work. And time for love. That leaves no other time. ~ *Coco Chanel*

16. Teamwork is the ability to work together toward a common vision. The ability to direct individual accomplishments toward organizational objectives. It is the fuel that allows

common people to attain uncommon results. ~ *Andrew Carnegie*

17. Nothing is particularly hard if you divide it into small jobs. ~ *Henry Ford*

18. I know the price of success: dedication, hard work and an unremitting devotion to the things you want to see happen. ~ *Frank Lloyd Wright*

19. Doing the best at this moment puts you in the best place for the next moment. ~ *Oprah Winfrey*

20. What is success? I think it is a mixture of having a flair for the thing that you are doing; knowing that it is not enough, that you have got to have hard work and a certain sense of purpose. ~ *Margaret Thatcher*

21. For every two minutes of glamour, there are eight hours of hard work. ~ *Jessica Savitch*

22. I've learned that anything in life worth having comes from patience and hard work. ~ *Greg Behrendt*

23. I learned the value of hard work by working hard. ~ *Margaret Mead*

_____

24. It takes a lot of unspectacular preparation to have spectacular results in both business and football. ~ *Roger Staubach*

_____

25. I work hard because I love my work. ~ *Bill Gates*

_____

26. Diamonds are nothing more than chunks of coal that stuck to their jobs. ~ *Malcolm Forbes*

_____

27. You must be very patient, very persistent. The world isn't going to shower gold coins on you just because you have a good idea. You're going to have to work like crazy to bring that idea to the attention of people. ~ Herb Kelleher

_____

28. If we win the hearts and minds of employees, we're going to have better business success. ~ Mary Barra

_____

29. The most important thing to do if you find yourself in a hole is to stop digging. ~ Warren Buffett

30. Just because you are a CEO, don't think you have landed. You must continually increase your learning, the way you think, and the way you approach the organization. I've never forgotten that. ~ Indra Nooyi

31. Success can be attained in any branch of human labor. There is always room at the top in every pursuit. ~ Andrew Carnegie

32. Growth and comfort do not coexist. ~ Ginni Rometty

33. You must be very patient, very persistent. The world isn't going to shower gold coins on you just because you have a good idea. You're going to have to work like crazy to bring that idea to the attention of people. ~ Herb Kelleher

34. If we win the hearts and minds of employees, we're going to have better business success. ~ Mary Barra

35. The most important thing to do if you find yourself in a hole is to stop digging. ~ Warren Buffett

36. Just because you are a CEO, don't think you have landed. You must continually increase your learning, the way you think, and the way you approach the organization. I've never forgotten that. ~ Indra Nooyi

37. Success can be attained in any branch of human labor. There is always room at the top in every pursuit. ~ Andrew Carnegie

38. Growth and comfort do not coexist. ~ Ginni Rometty

39. I knew that if I failed, I wouldn't regret that. But I knew the one thing I might regret is not trying. ~ Jeff Bezos

40. We need to accept that we won't always make the right decisions, that we'll screw up royally sometimes — understanding that failure is not the opposite of success, it's part of success. ~ Arianna Huffington

41. I'm convinced that about half of what separates the successful entrepreneurs from the non-successful ones is pure perseverance. ~ Steve Jobs

42. Do what you love and success will follow. Passion is the fuel behind a successful career. ~ Meg Whitman

43. The secret of success is to do the common thing uncommonly well." ~ John D. Rockefeller Jr

44. It is not necessary to do extraordinary things to get extraordinary results." ~ Warren Buffett

45. Before you are a leader, success is about growing yourself. When you become a leader, success is about growing others. ~ Jack Welch

46. Timing, perseverance, and ten years of trying will eventually make you look like an overnight success. ~ Biz Stone

47. Stay hungry, stay foolish. ~ Steve Jobs

48. Impossible is only an opinion. ~ Anik Singal

49. Even during a mid-life crisis do not deviate from your goal. History remembers only those who succeed. ~ Hockson Floin

50. I admire people who are very successful. But if that success has been achieved through too much ruthlessness, then I may admire that person, but I can't respect him. ~ Ratan Tata

51. Someone is sitting in the shade today because someone planted a tree a long time ago. ~ Warren Buffett

52. I never dreamed about success. I worked for it. ~ Estée Lauder

53. People often say that motivation doesn't last. Well, neither does bathing — that's why we recommend it daily. ~ Zig Ziglar

54. I owe my success to having listened respectfully to the very best advice, and then going away and doing the exact opposite. ~ G.K. Chesterton

---

55. If you really look closely, most overnight successes took a long time. ~ Steve Jobs

---

56. There are no secrets to success. It is the result of preparation, hard work and learning from failure. ~ Colin Powell

---

57. Success is often achieved by those who don't know that failure is inevitable. ~ Coco Chanel

---

58. There's no shortage of remarkable ideas, what's missing is the will to execute them. ~ Seth Godin

---

59. I don't know the word 'quit.' Either I never did, or I have abolished it. ~ Susan Butcher

---

60. Even if you are on the right track, you'll get run over if you just sit there. ~ Will Rodgers

61. The only way around is through. ~ Robert Frost

62. Success is not the key to happiness. Happiness is the key to success. If you love what you are doing, you will be successful. ~ Albert Schweitzer

63. The way to get started is to quit talking and begin doing. ~ Walt Disney

64. Whether you think you can or whether you think you can't, you're right! – Henry Ford

65. I feel that luck is preparation meeting opportunity. ~ Oprah Winfrey

66. Success is not final; failure is not fatal: it is the courage to continue that counts. ~ Winston Churchill

67. Forget past mistakes. Forget failures. Forget everything except what you're going to do now and do it. ~ William Durant

68. Many of life's failures are people who did not realize how close they were to success when they gave up. ~ Thomas Edison

69. Business opportunities are like buses, there's always another one coming. ~ Richard Branson

70. Success usually comes to those who are too busy to be looking for it. ~ Henry David Thoreau

71. None of us is as smart as all of us. ~ Ken Blanchard

72. True leadership lies in guiding others to success–in ensuring that everyone is performing at their best, doing the work they are pledged to do and doing it well. ~ Bill Owens

73. Management is doing things right; leadership is doing the right things. ~ Peter Drucker

74. Every time you have to speak, you are auditioning for leadership. ~ James Humes

75. One of the tests of leadership is the ability to recognize a problem before it becomes an emergency. ~ Arnold Glasow

76. The single biggest way to impact an organization is to focus on leadership development. There is almost no limit to the potential of an organization that recruits good people, raises them up as leaders and continually develops them. ~ John Maxwell

77. Becoming a leader is synonymous with becoming yourself. It is precisely that simple and it is also that difficult. ~ Warren Bennis

78. The function of leadership is to produce more leaders, not more followers. ~ Ralph Nader

79. Before you are a leader, success is all about growing yourself. When you become a leader, success is all about growing others. ~ Jack Welch

80. Its' fine to celebrate success, but it's more important to heed the lessons of failure. ~ Bill Gates

81. When you find an idea that you just can't stop thinking about, that's probably a good one to pursue. ~ Josh James

82. Success depends on employees. For me knowing and connecting with my employees is very important. ~ Divine Ndhlukula

83. Make something people want, including making a company that people want to work for. ~ Sahil Lavingia

84. Be undeniably good. No marketing effort or social media buzzword can be a substitute for that. ~ Anthony Volodkin

85. Always look for the fool in the deal. If you don't find one, it's you. ~ Mark Cuban

86. If you hire only those people you understand, the company will never get people better than you are. Always remember that you often find outstanding people among those you don't particularly like. ~ Soichiro Honda

87. If you define yourself by how you differ from the competition, you're probably in trouble. ~ Omar Hamoui

88. If you just work on stuff that you like and you're passionate about, you don't have to have a master plan with how things will play out. ~ Mark Zuckerberg

89. Every time we launch a feature, people yell at us. ~ Angelo Sotira

90. Be courageous – Look for opportunities to put your hand up and have a go. Back yourself. ~ Gail Kelly

91. Chase the vision, not the money, the money will end up following you. ~ Tony Hsieh

92. Your most unhappy customers are your greatest source of learning. ~ Bill Gates

93. Make every detail perfect and limit the number of details to perfect." ~ Jack Dorsey

94. There is no greater thing you can do with your life and your work than follow your passions – in a way that serves the world and you. ~ Richard Branson

95. Get five or six of your smartest friends in a room and ask them to rate your idea. ~ Mark Pincus

96. Your employees come first. And if you treat your employees right, guess what? Your customers come back, and that makes your shareholders happy. Start with employees and the rest follows from that. ~ Herb Kelleher

97. If you are not embarrassed by the first version of your product, you've launched too late. ~ Reid Hoffman

98. Your time is limited, so don't waste it living someone else's life. ~ Steve Jobs

99. Always deliver more than expected. ~ Larry Page

100. What do you need to start a business? Three simple things: know your product better than anyone, know your

customer, and have a burning desire to succeed. ~ Dave Thomas

---

101. Always think outside the box and embrace opportunities that appear, wherever they might be. ~ Lakshmi Mittal

---

102. Get big quietly, so you don't tip off potential competitors. ~ Chris Dixon

---

103. To retain the loyalty of those who are present, be loyal to those who are absent. ~ Stephen R. Covey

---

104. Entrepreneur is someone who has a vision for something and a want to create. ~ David Karp

---

105. In the end, a vision without the ability to execute it is probably a hallucination. ~ Steve Case

---

106. Empower yourself and realize the importance of contributing to the world by living your talent. Work on what you love. You are responsible for the talent that has been entrusted to you. ~ Catharina Bruns

107. It's not about ideas. It's about making ideas happen. ~ Scott Belsky

108. I don't look to jump over 7-foot bars — I look for 1-foot bars that I can step over. ~ Warren Buffett

109. The important thing is not being afraid to take a chance. Remember, the greatest failure is to not try. Once you find something you love to do, be the best at doing it. ~ Debbi Fields

110. Don't let others convince you that the idea is good when your gut tells you it's bad. ~ Kevin Rose

111. Everything started as nothing. ~ Ben Weissenstein

112. Risk more than others think is safe. Dream more than others think is practical. ~ Howard Schultz

113. Don't be afraid to assert yourself, have confidence in your abilities and don't let the bastards get you down. ~ Michael Bloomberg

114. Don't limit yourself. Many people limit themselves to what they think they can do. You can go as far as your mind lets

you. What you believe, remember, you can achieve. ~ Mary Kay Ash

115. You have to see failure as the beginning and the middle, but never entertain it as an end. ~ Jessica Herrin

116. The only thing worse than starting something and failing… is not starting something. ~ Seth Godin

117. When you are building a startup, it's difficult. Particularly, a startup that is expanding at the rate of Tinder. You have to give 100%, and you have to be committed. Solving the problem has to be personal or else you're going to disintegrate. ~ Sean Rad

118. If we tried to think of a good idea, we wouldn't have been able to think of a good idea. You just have to find the solution for a problem in your own life. ~ Brian Chesky

119. I cannot give you the formula for success, but I can give you the formula for failure, which is: Try to please everybody. ~ Herbert Swope

120. Outstanding leaders go out of their way to boost the self-esteem of their personnel. If people believe in themselves, it's amazing what they can accomplish. ~ Sam Walton

121. If your actions inspire others to dream more, learn more, do more and become more, you are a leader. ~ John Quincy Adams

122. Great leaders are willing to sacrifice the numbers to save the people. Poor leaders sacrifice the people to save the numbers. ~ Simon Sinek

123. Management is focusing on getting someone to get a result. Leadership is producing a standard in someone that when you're gone, they will live by to produce higher level results consistently. ~ Tony Robbins

124. Leadership does not always wear the harness of compromise. ~ Woodrow Wilson

125. Leadership is the capacity to translate vision into reality. ~ Warren Bennis

126. Don't find fault, find a remedy. ~ Henry Ford

127. Leadership is knowing when to lean on others and let them step up and shine. ~ Michelle Peluso

128. Google only loves you when everyone else loves you first. ~ Wendy Piersall

129. If your content isn't driving conversation, you're doing it wrong. ~ Dan Roth

130. Content is king but engagement is queen, and the lady rules the house! ~ Mari Smith

131. If you build it ... you may still need Google AdWords. ~ Jennifer Mesenbrink

132. If you can't explain it to a 6-year-old, you don't know it yourself. ~ Albert Einstein

133. Nothing great was ever achieved without enthusiasm. ~ Ralph Waldo Emerson

134. "Think big and don't listen to people who tell you it can't be done. Life's too short to think small." ~ Tim Ferriss

135. Failure is simply the opportunity to begin again, this time more intelligently. ~ Henry Ford

136. If you don't have room to fail, you don't have room to grow. ~ Jonathan Mildenhall

137. If something is important enough, even if the odds are against you, you should still do it. ~ Elon Musk

138. Risk more than others think is safe. Dream more than others think is practical. ~ Howard Schultz

139. It's easy to come up with new ideas; the hard part is letting go of what worked for you two years ago, but will soon be out of date. ~ Roger von Oech

140. Failure is another stepping stone to greatness. ~ Oprah Winfrey

141. Your attitude, not your aptitude, will determine your altitude. ~ Zig Ziglar

142. The best way to predict the future is to create it. ~ Peter Drucker

143. Creativity is intelligence having fun. ~ Albert Einstein

144. Ideas are easy. Implementation is hard. ~ Guy Kawasaki

145. Creativity, as has been said, consists largely of rearranging what we know in order to find out what we do not know. Hence, to think creatively, we must be able to look afresh at what we normally take for granted. ~ George Kneller

146. An essential aspect of creativity is not being afraid to fail. ~ Edwin Land

147. Good marketing makes the company look smart. Great marketing makes the customer feel smart. ~ Joe Chernov

148. Whether B2B or B2C, I believe passionately that good marketing essentials are the same. We all are emotional beings looking for relevance, context and connection. ~ Beth Comstock

149. Marketing is no longer about the stuff that you make, but about the stories you tell. ~ Seth Godin

150. Marketing is really just about sharing your passion. ~ Michael Hyatt

151. One of the best ways to sabotage your content is to not tie it to your goals. Know why you're creating content. ~ Ellen Gomes

152. If you're a good marketing person, you have to be a little crazy. ~ Jim Metcalf

153. Marketing is telling the world you're a rock star. Content marketing is showing the world you are one. ~ Robert Rose

154. Good marketers see consumers as complete human beings with all the dimensions real people have. ~ Jonah Sachs

155. Stop selling. Start helping. ~ Zig Ziglar

156. When you say it, it's marketing. When they say it, it's social proof. ~ Andy Crestodina

157. Build it, and they will come' only works in the movies. Social media is a build it, nurture it, engage them and they may come and stay. ~ Seth Godin

158. Social media is about the people. Not about your business. Provide for the people and the people will provide for you." ~ Matt Goulart

159. Social media is a contact sport. ~ Margaret Molloy

160. Activate your fans, don't just collect them like baseball cards. ~ Jay Baer

161. A brand is no longer what we tell the consumer it is — it is what consumers tell each other it is." ~ Scott Cook

162. Making promises and keeping them is a great way to build a brand. ~ Seth Godin

163. Your brand is a story unfolding across all customer touch points. ~ Jonah Sachs

164. If you're not failing now and again, it's a sign you're not doing anything innovative. ~ Woody Allen

165. If you're not stubborn, you'll give up on experiments too soon. And if you're not flexible, you'll pound your head against the wall and you won't see a different solution to a problem you're trying to solve. ~ Jeff Bezos

166. I'd rather apologize than to be so timid as to never try to do anything smart or brave. ~ Lee Clow

167. If you're looking for the next big thing, and you're looking where everyone else is, you're looking in the wrong place. ~ Mark Cuban

168. If you do what you've always done, you'll get what you've always gotten. ~ Tony Robbins

169. New ideas are sometimes found in the most granular details of a problem where few others bother to look. ~ Nate Silver

170. If your actions inspire others to dream more, learn more, do more and become more, you're a leader. ~ John Quincy Adams

171. Inspiration doesn't respond to meeting requests. You can't schedule greatness. ~ Jay Baer

172. As we look ahead into the next century, leaders will be those who empower others. ~ Bill Gates

173. The greatest leader is not necessarily the one who does the greatest things. He is the one that gets the people to do the greatest things. ~ Ronald Reagan

174. Do not follow where the path may lead. Go instead where there is no path and leave a trail. ~ Ralph Waldo Emerson

175. The very essence of leadership is that you have to have vision. You can't blow an uncertain trumpet. ~ Theodore M. Hesburgh

176. Every saint has a past... every sinner has a future. ~ Oscar Wilde

177. The pessimist complains about the wind. The optimist expects it to change. The leader adjusts the sails. ~ John Maxwell

178. A good objective of leadership is to help those who are doing poorly to do well and to help those who are doing well to do even better. ~ Jim Rohn

179. The role of most leaders is to get the people to think more of the leader but the role of the exceptional leader is to get the people to think more of themselves. ~ Booker T. Washington

180. Don't aim for success if you want it; just do what you love and believe in, and it will come naturally. ~ David Frost

181. In business, successful people reach goals, not quotas. ~ Stephen Jermyn

182. Failure is the condiment that gives success it's flavor. ~ Truman Capote

183. Success is not the key to happiness. Happiness is the key to success. If you love what you are doing, you will be successful. ~ Herman Cain

184. You always pass failure on your way to success. ~ Mickey Rooney

185. The best revenge is massive success. ~ Frank Sinatra

186. Desire is the key to motivation, but it's determination and commitment to an unrelenting pursuit of your goal - a

commitment to excellence - that will enable you to attain the success you seek. ~ Mario Andretti

187. Teamwork is the ability to work together toward a common vision. The ability to direct individual accomplishments toward organizational objectives. It is the fuel that allows common people to attain uncommon results. ~ Andrew Carnegie

188. Being a great teammate is work, hard work. It requires intention and discipline, just like becoming a better hitter or a better salesperson. But it is a skill set that I believe others, like me, can learn. ~ David Ross

189. It's not about working hard, it's about working together. You have to care more about the team than you do about yourself. ~ John Calipari

190. I'm a success today because I had a friend who believed in me and I didn't have the heart to let him down. ~ Abraham Lincoln

191. How far you go in life depends on your being tender with the young, compassionate with the aged, sympathetic with the striving and tolerant of the weak and strong. Because

someday in your life you will have been all of these. ~ George Washington Carver

192. I decided a long time ago that if I was going to hold grudges in business, it would turn into a full-time job. ~ LaVell Edwards

193. Ability is what you're capable of doing. Motivation determines what you do. Attitude determines how well you do it. ~ Lou Holtz

194. Have a fierce resolve in everything you do. Demonstrate determination, resiliency, and tenacity. Do not let temporary setbacks become permanent excuses. Use mistakes and problems as opportunities to get better-not reasons to quit. ~ Jamie Dimon

195. We are surrounded every day by people who do thankless but important work. ~ Brian Kilmeade

196. Discipline is the highest form of love. If you really love someone, you have to give them the level of discipline they need. ~ Tom Izzo

197. The hardest habit to develop is to win. The people who develop this habit never take winning for granted, they never feel entitled to victory. ~ Mike Krzyzewski

198. If we study what is merely average, we will remain merely average. ~ Shawn Achor

199. A winner is someone who can look in the mirror at the end of the day and say in pursuit of my goal and dreams I gave my best. ~ Dick Vitale

200. Every day we have an opportunity to create a living masterpiece. ~ Michael Gervais

201. Only those who dare to fail greatly can ever achieve greatly. ~ Robert F. Kennedy

202. A grateful heart is a beginning of greatness. It is an expression of humility. It is a foundation for the development of such virtues as prayer, faith, courage, contentment, happiness, love, and well-being. ~ James E. Faust

203. Be not afraid of greatness. Some are born great, some achieve greatness, and others have greatness thrust upon them. ~ William Shakespeare

---

204. All possibilities are on the other side of Yes. You have to have a Yes mindset to get to Greatness. ~ John C. Maxwell

---

205. When you're good at something, you'll tell everyone. When you're great at something, they'll tell you. ~ Walter Payton

---

206. Keep away from people who try to belittle your ambitions. Small people always try to do that, but the really great make you feel that you, too, are great. ~ Mark Twain

---

THE END.

www.ingramcontent.com/pod-product-compliance
Lightning Source LLC
Chambersburg PA
CBHW080547220526
45466CB00010B/3063